30 Beautiful VALUES To learn from THE QURAN

All rights reserved.

No part of this book may be reproduced, transmitted, or stored in an information retrieval system in any form or by any means, graphic, electronic, or mechanical, including photocopying, taping, and recording, without prior written permission from the author.

Copyright © 2022 GoodHearted Books Inc. (info@goodheartedbooks.com)

ISBN: 978-1-988779-49-2

Dépôt légal : bibliothèque et archives nationales du Québec, 2022.
Dépôt légal : bibliothèque et archives Canada, 2022.

Created by	: Bachar Karroum
Graphic Designer	: Samuel Gabriel
Cover Designer	: Creative Hands
Content revision	: Mohammed Achkanou, Safa Said, Mohamed Ali
Proofreader	: Amina Ahmed
Quran english version	: The Clear Quran (Dr. Khattab), Clear Quran (Talal Itani)

In the Name of God

Bringing this practical book to life for you and your little ones has been an inspiring journey. We are grateful to be able to build on our series of books to share the essence of Islam with kids. This creation has been specially crafted to shine a light on the beautiful wisdom of the Quran.

Through these pages, your child will uncover the precious and timeless values that come from the Quran, and will be equipped to apply these learnings in their day-to-day life. It is our wish that these pages will allow your little one to embrace their faith, connect with Allah through Dua, and absorb essential moral values that promote lifelong personal growth.

We hope that you and your family members will enjoy this learning experience, and that it will help your children become the best version of themselves, while spreading the wonderful values of our beloved religion.

Glossary

- Allah — Arabic word for God
- Al-Hamdoullillah — Praise be to God
- Bismillah — In the Name of God
- Dua — Asking Allah for blessings upon yourself and others
- PBUH — Peace be upon him
- Salam — Peace

 # START WITH BISMILLAH

Be positive

📖 WHAT THE HOLY QURAN TELLS US ABOUT THIS

(216) (...) Perhaps you dislike something which is good for you and like something which is bad for you. Allah knows and you do not know.

Al-Baqarah (The Cow) 2.216 Revealed in Madinah

(...)وَعَسَىٰ أَنْ تَكْرَهُوا شَيْئًا وَهُوَ خَيْرٌ لَكُمْ ۖ وَعَسَىٰ أَنْ تُحِبُّوا شَيْئًا وَهُوَ شَرٌّ لَكُمْ ۗ وَاللَّهُ يَعْلَمُ وَأَنْتُمْ لَا تَعْلَمُونَ ۝

♡ ♡ ♡ **DAY # 01** ♡ ♡ ♡

✦ I CAN LEARN FROM THE QURAN

Sometimes we don't realize that a negative experience or something we don't enjoy is good for us. What Allah knows, we may not see immediately. Embrace every situation.

🌿 TO BECOME A BETTER PERSON

Being positive helps strengthen my faith and build my confidence. It helps me to face any difficult situation with bravery and courage.

♡ WITH THE HELP OF ALLAH

O, Allah! Enlighten me when I may not see the benefit of a difficult situation.

END WITH AL-HAMDOULLILLAH ☾

♡ ♡ ♡ **DAY # 01** ♡ ♡ ♡

START WITH BISMILLAH

Honor your parents

📖 WHAT THE HOLY QURAN TELLS US ABOUT THIS

(23) Your Lord has commanded that you worship none but Him, and that you be good to your parents. If either of them or both of them reach old age with you, do not say to them a word of disrespect, nor scold them, but say to them kind words.

Al-Israa (The Night Journey) 17.23 Revealed in Makkah

وَقَضَىٰ رَبُّكَ أَلَّا تَعْبُدُوا إِلَّا إِيَّاهُ وَبِالْوَالِدَيْنِ إِحْسَانًا ۚ إِمَّا يَبْلُغَنَّ عِنْدَكَ الْكِبَرَ أَحَدُهُمَا أَوْ كِلَاهُمَا فَلَا تَقُلْ لَهُمَا أُفٍّ وَلَا تَنْهَرْهُمَا وَقُلْ لَهُمَا قَوْلًا كَرِيمًا ۝

DAY # 02

✨ I CAN LEARN FROM THE QURAN

Allah wants us to respect and honor our parents. We may not always like or understand the restrictions given by our parents. Even during these moments, we should remember to be good to our parents, never rude, and reply with respect.

🌿 TO BECOME A BETTER PERSON

Honoring my parents means showing them respect, and giving them all my love, even when I am upset. This helps me to build my understanding and keep my heart happy.

♡ WITH THE HELP OF ALLAH

O, Allah! Help me to love, support, and respect my parents.

END WITH AL-HAMDOULLILLAH 🌙

DAY # 02

START WITH BISMILLAH

Be open-hearted

📖 WHAT THE HOLY QURAN TELLS US ABOUT THIS

(8) But as for the one who came to you, eager 'to learn', (9) being in awe 'of Allah', (10) you were inattentive to him. (11) But no! This 'revelation' is truly a reminder. (12) So let whoever wills be mindful of it.

Abasa (He Frowned) 80.8-12 Revealed in Makkah

وَأَمَّا مَن جَاءَكَ يَسْعَىٰ ۝ وَهُوَ يَخْشَىٰ ۝ فَأَنتَ عَنْهُ تَلَهَّىٰ ۝ كَلَّا إِنَّهَا تَذْكِرَةٌ ۝ فَمَن شَاءَ ذَكَرَهُ ۝

♡ ♡ ♡ DAY # 03 ♡ ♡ ♡

✦ I CAN LEARN FROM THE QURAN

Allah wants us to keep our hearts open. We should never ignore or turn away someone who is looking for our friendship, needs help or reaches out to learn.

🌿 TO BECOME A BETTER PERSON

Keeping my arms and heart open to others helps me to build strong relationships. Others know that I can be counted on.

♡ WITH THE HELP OF ALLAH

O, Allah! Please help me to open my heart to everyone.

END WITH AL-HAMDOULLILLAH ☾

♡ ♡ ♡ **DAY # 03** ♡ ♡ ♡

START WITH BISMILLAH

Be grateful

📖 WHAT THE HOLY QURAN TELLS US ABOUT THIS

(7) And 'remember' when your Lord proclaimed, 'If you are grateful, I will certainly give you more (…)'.

Ibrahim (Ibrahim) 14.7 Revealed in Makkah

وَإِذْ تَأَذَّنَ رَبُّكُمْ لَئِن شَكَرْتُمْ لَأَزِيدَنَّكُمْ (...) ۝

♡ ♡ ♡ DAY # 04 ♡ ♡ ♡

✦ I CAN LEARN FROM THE QURAN

Allah emphasizes the importance of gratitude. When we are grateful, He increases our blessings. We should be thankful to the Almighty for everything that we have.

🌱 TO BECOME A BETTER PERSON

When I am grateful, I keep my heart full of love. Gratitude helps me get closer to Allah.

♡ WITH THE HELP OF ALLAH

O, Allah! May I always give you thanks and be grateful for all that we have.

END WITH AL-HAMDOULLILLAH ☾

♡ ♡ ♡ **DAY # 04** ♡ ♡ ♡

START WITH BISMILLAH

Give for the sake of Allah

📖 **WHAT THE HOLY QURAN TELLS US ABOUT THIS**

(264) O you who believe! Do not nullify your charitable deeds with reminders and hurtful words, like him who spends his wealth to be seen by the people, and does not believe in Allah and the Last Day (...).

Al-Baqarah (The Cow) 2.264 Revealed in Madinah

يَا أَيُّهَا الَّذِينَ آمَنُوا لَا تُبْطِلُوا صَدَقَاتِكُمْ بِالْمَنِّ وَالْأَذَىٰ كَالَّذِي يُنْفِقُ مَالَهُ رِئَاءَ النَّاسِ وَلَا يُؤْمِنُ بِاللَّهِ وَالْيَوْمِ الْآخِرِ (...) ﴿٢٦٤﴾

♡ ♡ ♡ **DAY # 05** ♡ ♡ ♡

✦ I CAN LEARN FROM THE QURAN

We should always observe our intention before doing any good deed or giving charity. We should not do charitable deeds to show off or seek a good reputation. Reminding others of the charity or the favors we provided them is like we have not done any of them.

🌿 TO BECOME A BETTER PERSON

Giving without expecting anything in return helps me to be generous and makes me feel good.

♡ WITH THE HELP OF ALLAH

O, Allah! Accept my charities and favors, and protect me from showing them off.

END WITH AL-HAMDOULLILLAH ☾

♡ ♡ ♡ **DAY # 05** ♡ ♡ ♡

START WITH BISMILLAH

Embrace diversity and inclusion

📖 WHAT THE HOLY QURAN TELLS US ABOUT THIS

(13) O humanity! Indeed, We created you from a male and a female, and made you into peoples and tribes so that you may 'get to' know one another. Surely the most noble of you in the sight of Allah is the most righteous among you (...).

Al-Hujurat (The Rooms) 49.13 Revealed in Madinah

يَا أَيُّهَا النَّاسُ إِنَّا خَلَقْنَاكُم مِّن ذَكَرٍ وَأُنثَىٰ وَجَعَلْنَاكُمْ شُعُوبًا وَقَبَائِلَ لِتَعَارَفُوا ۚ إِنَّ أَكْرَمَكُمْ عِندَ اللَّهِ أَتْقَاكُمْ (...) ﴿١٣﴾

♡ ♡ ♡ **DAY # 06** ♡ ♡ ♡

✩ I CAN LEARN FROM THE QURAN

Allah created everyone equally. We should never discriminate based on gender, color, status, or for any other reason.

🌿 TO BECOME A BETTER PERSON

When I respect every human being, no matter their color or the language they speak, I set an example. I contribute to spreading positivity, and I embrace diversity and inclusion.

♡ WITH THE HELP OF ALLAH

O, Allah! Make me respect every human being.

END WITH AL-HAMDOULLILLAH ☾

DAY # 06

START WITH BISMILLAH

Always tell the truth

📖 WHAT THE HOLY QURAN TELLS US ABOUT THIS

(70) O believers! Be mindful of Allah, and say what is right. (71) He will bless your deeds for you, and forgive your sins. And whoever obeys Allah and His Messenger, has truly achieved a great triumph.

Al-Ahzab (The Combined Forces) 33.70-71 Revealed in Madinah

يَا أَيُّهَا الَّذِينَ آمَنُوا اتَّقُوا اللَّهَ وَقُولُوا قَوْلًا سَدِيدًا ۝ يُصْلِحْ لَكُمْ أَعْمَالَكُمْ وَيَغْفِرْ لَكُمْ ذُنُوبَكُمْ ۗ وَمَنْ يُطِعِ اللَّهَ وَرَسُولَهُ فَقَدْ فَازَ فَوْزًا عَظِيمًا ۝

✨ I CAN LEARN FROM THE QURAN

Allah wants us to tell the truth, and never lie, whatever the situation may be. Sometimes, after a mistake, we may think that a lie will save us, but ultimately, lying will make us lose our credibility.

🌿 TO BECOME A BETTER PERSON

By always telling the truth, I become an honest and trustworthy person.

♡ WITH THE HELP OF ALLAH

O, Allah! Help me remain honest, and save me from telling lies in every situation.

END WITH AL-HAMDOULLILLAH 🌙

♡ ♡ ♡ **DAY # 07** ♡ ♡ ♡

START WITH BISMILLAH

Be humble

📖 WHAT THE HOLY QURAN TELLS US ABOUT THIS

(63) The servants of the Merciful are those who walk the earth in humility, and when the ignorant address them, they say, "Peace."

Al-Furqan (The Criterion) 25.63 Revealed in Makkah

وَعِبَادُ الرَّحْمَٰنِ الَّذِينَ يَمْشُونَ عَلَى الْأَرْضِ هَوْنًا وَإِذَا خَاطَبَهُمُ الْجَاهِلُونَ قَالُوا سَلَامًا ﴿٦٣﴾

♡ ♡ ♡ DAY # 08 ♡ ♡ ♡

✨ I CAN LEARN FROM THE QURAN

Allah highlights through this verse the importance of remaining humble, and that arrogance is never rewarded. We should avoid showing off our wealth and successes.

🌿 TO BECOME A BETTER PERSON

By remaining humble, I help build my self-confidence, and I don't get upset by the ignorance of others.

♡ WITH THE HELP OF ALLAH

O, Allah! Make me amongst your humble servants and give me the strength to speak words of peace when confronted by ignorance.

END WITH AL-HAMDOULLILLAH 🌙

START WITH BISMILLAH

Share your blessings

📖 WHAT THE HOLY QURAN TELLS US ABOUT THIS

(26) Give to close relatives their due, as well as the poor and 'needy' travellers. And do not spend wastefully.

Al-Israa (The Night Journey) 17.26 Revealed in Makkah

وَآتِ ذَا الْقُرْبَىٰ حَقَّهُ وَالْمِسْكِينَ وَابْنَ السَّبِيلِ وَلَا تُبَذِّرْ تَبْذِيرًا ﴿٢٦﴾

♡ ♡ ♡ DAY # 09 ♡ ♡ ♡

✧ I CAN LEARN FROM THE QURAN

Allah values sharing, and doesn't like us to waste things. If we have more than we need, we should share it with our relatives or with those in need. Allah will reward us for sharing.

🌿 TO BECOME A BETTER PERSON

By sharing, I demonstrate my love and care for others, and it makes my heart rejoice.

♡ WITH THE HELP OF ALLAH

O, Allah! Thank you for every blessing. Help me to share and be generous. Help me avoid wasting.

END WITH AL-HAMDOULLILLAH ☾

♡ ♡ ♡ **DAY # 09** ♡ ♡ ♡

START WITH BISMILLAH

Feed the ones in need

📖 WHAT THE HOLY QURAN TELLS US ABOUT THIS

(8) And they feed, for the love of Him, the poor, and the orphan, and the captive. (9) "We only feed you for the sake of Allah. We want from you neither compensation, nor gratitude."

Al-Insan (The Man) 76.8-9 Revealed in Madinah

وَيُطْعِمُونَ الطَّعَامَ عَلَىٰ حُبِّهِ مِسْكِينًا وَيَتِيمًا وَأَسِيرًا ﴿٨﴾ إِنَّمَا نُطْعِمُكُمْ لِوَجْهِ اللَّهِ لَا نُرِيدُ مِنكُمْ جَزَاءً وَلَا شُكُورًا ﴿٩﴾

♡ ♡ ♡ **DAY # 10** ♡ ♡ ♡

✦ I CAN LEARN FROM THE QURAN

Allah has appointed our duty to feed those who are in need. He has given us many blessings and an abundance of food. We should share and always try to provide for someone in need.

🌿 TO BECOME A BETTER PERSON

When I share my food, I help provide for those in need. Helping others brings me joy.

♡ WITH THE HELP OF ALLAH

O, Allah! Help me to have the ability to always feed someone in need.

END WITH AL-HAMDOULLILLAH ☾

♡ ♡ ♡ **DAY # 10** ♡ ♡ ♡

 # START WITH BISMILLAH

Avoid making assumptions

📖 WHAT THE HOLY QURAN TELLS US ABOUT THIS

(12) O you who have believed, avoid much [negative] assumption. Indeed, some assumption is sin. And do not spy or backbite each other (...)

Al-Hujurat (The Rooms) 49.12 Revealed in Madinah

يَا أَيُّهَا الَّذِينَ آمَنُوا اجْتَنِبُوا كَثِيرًا مِنَ الظَّنِّ إِنَّ بَعْضَ الظَّنِّ إِثْمٌ ۖ وَلَا تَجَسَّسُوا وَلَا يَغْتَب بَعْضُكُم بَعْضًا (...) ﴿١٢﴾

♡ ♡ ♡ DAY # 11 ♡ ♡ ♡

✩ I CAN LEARN FROM THE QURAN

Allah is telling us to avoid making assumptions. If we hear something negative about someone, we should pay attention and evaluate the information. We should not disclose it to others.

🌿 TO BECOME A BETTER PERSON

By avoiding making assumptions, I build my critical thinking. By not talking negatively about others in their absence, I nurture my honesty.

♡ WITH THE HELP OF ALLAH

O, Allah! Help me to avoid making assumptions.

END WITH AL-HAMDOULLILLAH ☾

♡ ♡ ♡ **DAY # 11** ♡ ♡ ♡

START WITH BISMILLAH

Control your anger, and forgive

WHAT THE HOLY QURAN TELLS US ABOUT THIS

(134) 'They are' those who donate in prosperity and adversity, control their anger, and pardon others. And Allah loves the good-doers.

Ali 'Imran (Family of Imran) 3.134 Revealed in Madinah

الَّذِينَ يُنْفِقُونَ فِي السَّرَّاءِ وَالضَّرَّاءِ وَالْكَاظِمِينَ الْغَيْظَ وَالْعَافِينَ عَنِ النَّاسِ ۗ وَاللَّهُ يُحِبُّ الْمُحْسِنِينَ ﴿١٣٤﴾

♡ ♡ ♡ **DAY # 12** ♡ ♡ ♡

✩ I CAN LEARN FROM THE QURAN

Allah loves doers of good. He praises those who control their anger and who forgive others. Feeling angry is normal, but controlling our anger is a virtue. We should avoid losing our temper and should not hold any grudges.

🌿 TO BECOME A BETTER PERSON

By controlling my anger, I help build my self-control and contribute to creating a positive environment. By forgiving others, I help keep my heart at peace.

♡ WITH THE HELP OF ALLAH

[O, Allah! Please help me to control my anger and be forgiving.]

END WITH AL-HAMDOULLILLAH 🌙

♡ ♡ ♡ **DAY # 12** ♡ ♡ ♡

START WITH BISMILLAH

Do not spread gossip

📖 WHAT THE HOLY QURAN TELLS US ABOUT THIS

(10) And do not obey any vile swearer. (11) Backbiter, spreader of slander. (12) Preventer of good, transgressor, sinner.

Al-Qalam (The Pen) 68.10-12 Revealed in Makkah

وَلَا تُطِعْ كُلَّ حَلَّافٍ مَهِينٍ ۝ هَمَّازٍ مَشَّاءٍ بِنَمِيمٍ ۝ مَنَّاعٍ لِلْخَيْرِ مُعْتَدٍ أَثِيمٍ ۝

♡ ♡ ♡ **DAY # 13** ♡ ♡ ♡

✨ I CAN LEARN FROM THE QURAN

Gossiping is not to be taken lightly. We should always speak frankly and avoid spreading rumors. We should be careful when we are not sure about a given matter.

🌿 TO BECOME A BETTER PERSON

By not engaging in gossip, I encourage positive conversations, and this helps my heart to remain pure.

♡ WITH THE HELP OF ALLAH

O, Allah! Protect me from spreading gossip, and forgive me if I do so unintentionally.

END WITH AL-HAMDOULLILLAH 🌙

♡ ♡ ♡ **DAY # 13** ♡ ♡ ♡

START WITH BISMILLAH

Assume the best in others

📖 WHAT THE HOLY QURAN TELLS US ABOUT THIS

(12) Why, when you heard about it, the believing men and women did not think well of one another, and say, "This is an obvious lie"?

An-Nur (The Light) 24.12 Revealed in Madinah

لَوْلَا إِذْ سَمِعْتُمُوهُ ظَنَّ الْمُؤْمِنُونَ وَالْمُؤْمِنَاتُ بِأَنْفُسِهِمْ خَيْرًا وَقَالُوا هَٰذَا إِفْكٌ مُبِينٌ ۝

♡ ♡ ♡ **DAY # 14** ♡ ♡ ♡

✧ I CAN LEARN FROM THE QURAN

Always see the good in others. We must remain critical when we hear negative comments, rumors, or calumnies about others.

🌿 TO BECOME A BETTER PERSON

By choosing to see the good in others, I empower myself. Always assuming the best in others builds my compassion and helps create a positive environment.

♡ WITH THE HELP OF ALLAH

O, Allah! Help me to stay positive, and don't let negativity enter my heart.

END WITH AL-HAMDOULLILLAH ☾

♡ ♡ ♡ **DAY # 14** ♡ ♡ ♡

START WITH BISMILLAH

Be hospitable

📖 WHAT THE HOLY QURAN TELLS US ABOUT THIS

(24) Has the story of Abraham's honorable guests reached you? (25) When they entered upon him, they said, "Peace." He said, "Peace, strangers." (26) Then he slipped away to his family, and brought a fatted calf. (27) He set it before them. He said, "Will you not eat?"

Adh-Dhariyat (The Winnowing Winds) 51.24-27 Revealed in Makkah

هَلْ أَتَاكَ حَدِيثُ ضَيْفِ إِبْرَاهِيمَ الْمُكْرَمِينَ ﴿٢٤﴾ إِذْ دَخَلُوا عَلَيْهِ فَقَالُوا سَلَامًا ۖ قَالَ سَلَامٌ قَوْمٌ مُنكَرُونَ ﴿٢٥﴾ فَرَاغَ إِلَىٰ أَهْلِهِ فَجَاءَ بِعِجْلٍ سَمِينٍ ﴿٢٦﴾ فَقَرَّبَهُ إِلَيْهِمْ قَالَ أَلَا تَأْكُلُونَ ﴿٢٧﴾

♡ ♡ ♡ DAY # 15 ♡ ♡ ♡

☆ I CAN LEARN FROM THE QURAN

The beautiful story of Prophet Ibrahim (PBUH) highlights how Allah wants us to welcome and treat our guests. We should honor their presence with Salam, offer them food, and invite them to eat.

🌱 TO BECOME A BETTER PERSON

By being hospitable, I let others know that they are important to me. It helps me to create and maintain positive relationships.

♡ WITH THE HELP OF ALLAH

[O, Allah! Let me be the best host for my guests.]

END WITH AL-HAMDOULLILLAH

START WITH BISMILLAH

Be respectful, do not make fun of people

📖 WHAT THE HOLY QURAN TELLS US ABOUT THIS

(11) O believers! Do not let some 'men' ridicule others, they may be better than them, nor let 'some' women ridicule other women, they may be better than them. Do not defame one another, nor call each other by offensive nicknames (...)

Al-Hujurat (The Rooms) 49.11 Revealed in Madinah

يَا أَيُّهَا الَّذِينَ آمَنُوا لَا يَسْخَرْ قَوْمٌ مِنْ قَوْمٍ عَسَىٰ أَنْ يَكُونُوا خَيْرًا مِنْهُمْ وَلَا نِسَاءٌ مِنْ نِسَاءٍ عَسَىٰ أَنْ يَكُنَّ خَيْرًا مِنْهُنَّ ۖ وَلَا تَلْمِزُوا أَنْفُسَكُمْ وَلَا تَنَابَزُوا بِالْأَلْقَابِ (...) ﴿١١﴾

♡ ♡ ♡ **DAY # 16** ♡ ♡ ♡

✨ I CAN LEARN FROM THE QURAN

Allah has forbidden us from insulting or making fun of people, calling anyone bad names, or ridiculing others' appearance. We should always respect one another. We may think we are better than others, but as Allah says, maybe they are better than us.

🌱 TO BECOME A BETTER PERSON

By respecting others and not insulting anyone, I am keeping my heart open. Respecting differences means I am inclusive and open-minded.

♡ WITH THE HELP OF ALLAH

O, Allah! Help me to respect others, and protect me from making fun of their weaknesses.

END WITH AL-HAMDOULLILLAH ☾

♡ ♡ ♡ **DAY # 16** ♡ ♡ ♡

START WITH BISMILLAH

Always do good

📖 WHAT THE HOLY QURAN TELLS US ABOUT THIS

(34) Good and evil cannot be equal. Respond 'to evil' with what is best, then the one you are in a feud with will be like a close friend.

Fussilat (Explained in Detail) 41.34 Revealed in Makkah

وَلَا تَسْتَوِي الْحَسَنَةُ وَلَا السَّيِّئَةُ ۚ ادْفَعْ بِالَّتِي هِيَ أَحْسَنُ فَإِذَا الَّذِي بَيْنَكَ وَبَيْنَهُ عَدَاوَةٌ كَأَنَّهُ وَلِيٌّ حَمِيمٌ ﴿٣٤﴾

♡ ♡ ♡ DAY # 17 ♡ ♡ ♡

✦ I CAN LEARN FROM THE QURAN

Good is greater than evil. We should always respond with good, even when others may hurt us.

🌿 TO BECOME A BETTER PERSON

When I focus on the good, it helps me to stay positive, happy, and in good spirits. Doing good helps me to reinforce my faith.

♡ WITH THE HELP OF ALLAH

O, Allah! Give me strength to always do good, even to those who may hurt me.

END WITH AL-HAMDOULLILLAH ☾

♡ ♡ ♡ **DAY # 17** ♡ ♡ ♡

START WITH BISMILLAH

Keep your promises

📖 WHAT THE HOLY QURAN TELLS US ABOUT THIS

(2) O you who believe! Why do you say what you do not do? (3) It is most hateful to Allah that you say what you do not do.

As-Saf (The Ranks) 61.2-3 Revealed in Madinah

يَا أَيُّهَا الَّذِينَ آمَنُوا لِمَ تَقُولُونَ مَا لَا تَفْعَلُونَ ۝ كَبُرَ مَقْتًا عِنْدَ اللَّهِ أَنْ تَقُولُوا مَا لَا تَفْعَلُونَ ۝

DAY # 18

✦ I CAN LEARN FROM THE QURAN

Allah asks that we never break a promise or trust. Stay true to our word. We should always keep our promises and not lose the trust that others place in us.

🌿 TO BECOME A BETTER PERSON

By keeping my promises, I become trustworthy.

♡ WITH THE HELP OF ALLAH

[O, Allah! Help me to always keep and fulfill my promises.]

END WITH AL-HAMDOULLILLAH ☾

♡ ♡ ♡ **DAY # 18** ♡ ♡ ♡

START WITH BISMILLAH

Spend or consume wisely

WHAT THE HOLY QURAN TELLS US ABOUT THIS

(67) And those who, when they spend, are neither wasteful nor stingy, but choose a middle course between that.

Al-Furqan (The Criterion) 25.67 Revealed in Makkah

وَالَّذِينَ إِذَا أَنْفَقُوا لَمْ يُسْرِفُوا وَلَمْ يَقْتُرُوا وَكَانَ بَيْنَ ذَٰلِكَ قَوَامًا ﴿٦٧﴾

DAY # 19

✨ I CAN LEARN FROM THE QURAN

Allah shares with us the importance of moderation in consumption. We must spend or consume wisely, not be extravagant or waste anything, yet not become a miser.

🌿 TO BECOME A BETTER PERSON

By spending wisely, I learn how to manage my priorities, and focus on what is truly important to me.

♡ WITH THE HELP OF ALLAH

O, Allah! Save me from the extremes and help me to consume wisely.

END WITH AL-HAMDOULLILLAH ☾

♡ ♡ ♡ **DAY # 19** ♡ ♡ ♡

START WITH BISMILLAH

Be knowledgeable

> 📖 **WHAT THE HOLY QURAN TELLS US ABOUT THIS**
>
> (114) Exalted is Allah, the True King! Do not rush to recite 'a revelation of' the Quran 'O Prophet' before it is 'properly' conveyed to you, and pray, "My Lord! Increase me in knowledge."

Taha (Ta-ha) 20.114 Revealed in Makkah

فَتَعَالَى اللَّهُ الْمَلِكُ الْحَقُّ ۗ وَلَا تَعْجَلْ بِالْقُرْآنِ مِن قَبْلِ أَن يُقْضَىٰ إِلَيْكَ وَحْيُهُ ۖ وَقُل رَّبِّ زِدْنِي عِلْمًا ﴿١١٤﴾

DAY # 20

✨ I CAN LEARN FROM THE QURAN

This is a beautiful Dua which Allah taught our Prophet Mohammad (PBUH) as he was learning to read the Quran. Whenever you face difficulty learning something new, keep at it. Know that you can ask Allah to assist you.

🌱 TO BECOME A BETTER PERSON

When I learn new things, I enhance my knowledge and nurture my curiosity. Even if it is difficult, I exercise my patience and persistence.

♡ WITH THE HELP OF ALLAH

O, Allah! Please give me wisdom and the curiosity to keep on learning.

END WITH AL-HAMDOULLILLAH ☾

♡ ♡ ♡ **DAY # 20** ♡ ♡ ♡

START WITH BISMILLAH

Return a greeting in a good manner

📖 WHAT THE HOLY QURAN TELLS US ABOUT THIS

(86) And when you are greeted, respond with a better greeting or at least similarly. Surely Allah is a 'vigilant' Reckoner of all things.

An-Nisa (The Women) 4.86 Revealed in Madinah

وَإِذَا حُيِّيتُم بِتَحِيَّةٍ فَحَيُّوا بِأَحْسَنَ مِنْهَا أَوْ رُدُّوهَا ۗ إِنَّ اللَّهَ كَانَ عَلَىٰ كُلِّ شَيْءٍ حَسِيبًا ﴿٨٦﴾

DAY # 21

✦ I CAN LEARN FROM THE QURAN

Good manners are important in the eyes of Allah. They represent an act of love. When we receive a greeting, we should demonstrate appreciation by responding with a better greeting, if possible.

🌿 TO BECOME A BETTER PERSON

By showing good manners and responding properly to greetings, I demonstrate gratitude and help to spread goodness around me.

♡ WITH THE HELP OF ALLAH

O, Allah! Please help me to return greetings properly and remain loving.

END WITH AL-HAMDOULLILLAH ☾

♡ ♡ ♡ **DAY # 21** ♡ ♡ ♡

START WITH BISMILLAH

Always stand for justice

📖 WHAT THE HOLY QURAN TELLS US ABOUT THIS

(135) O you who believe! Stand firmly for justice, as witnesses to Allah, even if against yourselves, or your parents, or your relatives. Whether one is rich or poor, Allah takes care of both (...).

An-Nisa (The Women) 4.135 Revealed in Madinah

يَا أَيُّهَا الَّذِينَ آمَنُوا كُونُوا قَوَّامِينَ بِالْقِسْطِ شُهَدَاءَ لِلَّهِ وَلَوْ عَلَىٰ أَنْفُسِكُمْ أَوِ الْوَالِدَيْنِ وَالْأَقْرَبِينَ إِنْ يَكُنْ غَنِيًّا أَوْ فَقِيرًا فَاللَّهُ أَوْلَىٰ بِهِمَا (...) ﴿١٣٥﴾

DAY # 22

✨ I CAN LEARN FROM THE QURAN

Justice is important to Allah. We should always stand by the truth, remain honest and acknowledge our mistakes. Allah loves fairness and asks that we stand by justice even when the truth could expose our loved ones.

🌿 TO BECOME A BETTER PERSON

Being just in every situation and with everyone, helps me do the right thing. It demonstrates my true love for others and keeps my heart pure.

♡ WITH THE HELP OF ALLAH

[O, Allah! Help me stay just in every situation.]

END WITH AL-HAMDOULLILLAH 🌙

♡ ♡ ♡ **DAY # 22** ♡ ♡ ♡

START WITH BISMILLAH

Appreciate every contribution, no matter how small

📖 WHAT THE HOLY QURAN TELLS US ABOUT THIS

(79) Those who criticize the believers who give charity voluntarily, and ridicule those who find nothing to give except their own efforts—Allah ridicules them (...).

At-Tawbah (The Repentance) 9.79 Revealed in Madinah

الَّذِينَ يَلْمِزُونَ الْمُطَّوِّعِينَ مِنَ الْمُؤْمِنِينَ فِي الصَّدَقَاتِ وَالَّذِينَ لَا يَجِدُونَ إِلَّا جُهْدَهُمْ فَيَسْخَرُونَ مِنْهُمْ ۗ سَخِرَ اللَّهُ مِنْهُمْ (...) ﴿٧٩﴾

DAY # 23

✦ I CAN LEARN FROM THE QURAN

In the eyes of Allah, even the smallest contribution has value. We should never criticize those who contribute small amounts to charity or make small efforts.

🌱 TO BECOME A BETTER PERSON

Respecting the efforts and contributions of others, no matter how small they are, builds my empathy and reinforces my kindness.

♡ WITH THE HELP OF ALLAH

O, Allah! Protect me from criticizing others' contributions or making fun of their efforts.

END WITH AL-HAMDOULLILLAH ☾

♡ ♡ ♡ **DAY # 23** ♡ ♡ ♡

START WITH BISMILLAH

Validate the truth, don't accuse without evidence

📖 WHAT THE HOLY QURAN TELLS US ABOUT THIS

(6) O you who believe! If a troublemaker brings you any news, investigate, lest you harm people out of ignorance, and you become regretful for what you have done.

Al-Hujurat (The Rooms) 49.6 Revealed in Madinah

يَا أَيُّهَا الَّذِينَ آمَنُوا إِنْ جَاءَكُمْ فَاسِقٌ بِنَبَإٍ فَتَبَيَّنُوا أَنْ تُصِيبُوا قَوْمًا بِجَهَالَةٍ فَتُصْبِحُوا عَلَىٰ مَا فَعَلْتُمْ نَادِمِينَ ﴿٦﴾

DAY # 24

✦ I CAN LEARN FROM THE QURAN

Allah has forbidden us from accusing anyone without proof. We shall not judge and never accuse, without evidence.

🌿 TO BECOME A BETTER PERSON

Validating the truth, and not accusing without evidence, helps me to build my critical thinking.

♡ WITH THE HELP OF ALLAH

O, Allah! Help me to see clearly, so that I don't falsely accuse anyone.

END WITH AL-HAMDOULLILLAH ☾

♡ ♡ ♡ **DAY # 24** ♡ ♡ ♡

START WITH BISMILLAH

Respect the belongings of others

📖 WHAT THE HOLY QURAN TELLS US ABOUT THIS

(29) O you who believe! Do not consume each other's wealth illicitly, but trade by mutual consent. And do not kill yourselves, for Allah is Merciful towards you.

An-Nisa (The Women) 4.29 Revealed in Madinah

يَا أَيُّهَا الَّذِينَ آمَنُوا لَا تَأْكُلُوا أَمْوَالَكُمْ بَيْنَكُمْ بِالْبَاطِلِ إِلَّا أَنْ تَكُونَ تِجَارَةً عَنْ تَرَاضٍ مِنْكُمْ ۚ وَلَا تَقْتُلُوا أَنْفُسَكُمْ ۚ إِنَّ اللَّهَ كَانَ بِكُمْ رَحِيمًا ﴿٢٩﴾

DAY # 25

✦ I CAN LEARN FROM THE QURAN

Allah has asked us not to cheat or take advantage of anyone's wealth. We should respect the belongings of others.

🌿 TO BECOME A BETTER PERSON

Respecting other people's belongings helps me to remain honest. It helps me to reinforce my gratitude towards my belongings.

♡ WITH THE HELP OF ALLAH

O, Allah! Save me from taking advantage of the wealth and situation of others.

END WITH AL-HAMDOULLILLAH ☾

♡ ♡ ♡ **DAY # 25** ♡ ♡ ♡

START WITH BISMILLAH

Be forgiving

📖 WHAT THE HOLY QURAN TELLS US ABOUT THIS

(22) Do not let the people of virtue and affluence among you swear to suspend donations to their relatives, the needy, and the emigrants in the cause of Allah. Let them pardon and forgive (...).

An-Nur (The Light) 24.22 Revealed in Madinah

وَلَا يَأْتَلِ أُولُو الْفَضْلِ مِنْكُمْ وَالسَّعَةِ أَنْ يُؤْتُوا أُولِي الْقُرْبَىٰ وَالْمَسَاكِينَ وَالْمُهَاجِرِينَ فِي سَبِيلِ اللَّهِ ۖ وَلْيَعْفُوا وَلْيَصْفَحُوا ﴿٢٢﴾

DAY # 26

✦ I CAN LEARN FROM THE QURAN

Allah values forgiveness. We should forgive others in the same way we would like Allah and others to forgive us.

🌱 TO BECOME A BETTER PERSON

Forgiving keeps my heart pure and free from all worry. It also helps me to maintain healthy relationships.

♡ WITH THE HELP OF ALLAH

O, Allah! Remind me of your greatness, and to be forgiving of others, just as You are with me.

END WITH AL-HAMDOULLILLAH ☾

♡ ♡ ♡ **DAY # 26** ♡ ♡ ♡

START WITH BISMILLAH

Lead by example

WHAT THE HOLY QURAN TELLS US ABOUT THIS

(44) Do you preach righteousness and fail to practice it yourselves, although you read the Scripture? Do you not understand?

Al-Baqarah (The Cow) 2.44 Revealed in Madinah

أَتَأْمُرُونَ النَّاسَ بِالْبِرِّ وَتَنْسَوْنَ أَنْفُسَكُمْ وَأَنْتُمْ تَتْلُونَ الْكِتَابَ أَفَلَا تَعْقِلُونَ ﴿٤٤﴾

DAY # 27

✧ I CAN LEARN FROM THE QURAN

Allah asks that we practice what we preach. We cannot ask someone to behave properly or do something if we don't do so ourselves.

🌱 TO BECOME A BETTER PERSON

Practicing what I preach helps me to develop and nurture my authenticity.

♡ WITH THE HELP OF ALLAH

O, Allah! Give me strength and wisdom to be a good example to others.

END WITH AL-HAMDOULLILLAH ☾

♡ ♡ ♡ **DAY # 27** ♡ ♡ ♡

START WITH BISMILLAH

Be patient

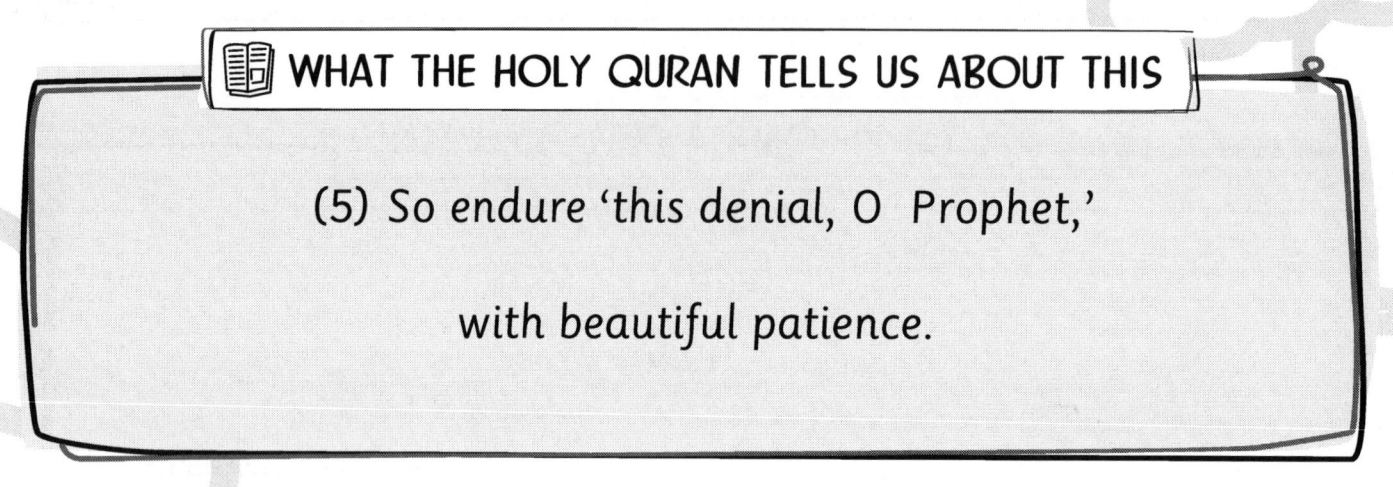

📖 WHAT THE HOLY QURAN TELLS US ABOUT THIS

(5) So endure 'this denial, O Prophet,' with beautiful patience.

Al-Ma'arij (The Ascending Stairways) 70.5 Revealed in Makkah

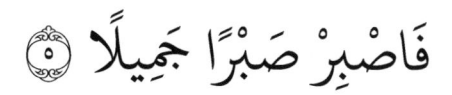

فَاصْبِرْ صَبْرًا جَمِيلًا ﴿٥﴾

♥ ♥ ♥ DAY # 28 ♥ ♥ ♥

✧ I CAN LEARN FROM THE QURAN

Allah asks that we remain patient in all circumstances. We must always trust Allah's guidance.

🌿 TO BECOME A BETTER PERSON

Being patient helps me make thoughtful decisions, and build my judgment and tolerance. It helps me grow my inner strength.

♡ WITH THE HELP OF ALLAH

O, Allah! Give me patience in all circumstances.

END WITH AL-HAMDOULLILLAH ☾

♡ ♡ ♡ **DAY # 28** ♡ ♡ ♡

START WITH BISMILLAH

Be kind

📖 **WHAT THE HOLY QURAN TELLS US ABOUT THIS**

(28) But if you must turn them down 'because you lack the means to give'—while hoping to receive your Lord's bounty—then 'at least' give them a kind word.

Al-Israa (The Night Journey) 17.28 Revealed in Makkah

وَإِمَّا تُعْرِضَنَّ عَنْهُمُ ابْتِغَاءَ رَحْمَةٍ مِنْ رَبِّكَ تَرْجُوهَا فَقُلْ لَهُمْ قَوْلًا مَيْسُورًا ﴿٢٨﴾

♡ ♡ ♡ **DAY # 29** ♡ ♡ ♡

✦ I CAN LEARN FROM THE QURAN

Allah asks that we speak kindly to everyone, especially to the ones in need. Even if we have nothing to give, we should be kind and offer words of comfort.

🌿 TO BECOME A BETTER PERSON

Being kind makes others happy, and it helps me build my empathy.

♡ WITH THE HELP OF ALLAH

[O, Allah! Please fill my heart with kindness.]

END WITH AL-HAMDOULLILLAH ☾

♡ ♡ ♡ DAY # 29 ♡ ♡ ♡

START WITH BISMILLAH

Think critically and act with clarity

📖 WHAT THE HOLY QURAN TELLS US ABOUT THIS

(6) O you who believe! If a troublemaker brings you any news, investigate, lest you harm people out of ignorance, and you become regretful for what you have done.

Al-Hujurat (The Rooms) 49.6 Revealed in Madinah

يَا أَيُّهَا الَّذِينَ آمَنُوا إِنْ جَاءَكُمْ فَاسِقٌ بِنَبَإٍ فَتَبَيَّنُوا أَنْ تُصِيبُوا قَوْمًا بِجَهَالَةٍ فَتُصْبِحُوا عَلَىٰ مَا فَعَلْتُمْ نَادِمِينَ ﴿٦﴾

DAY # 30

✩ I CAN LEARN FROM THE QURAN

Allah wants us to always validate the source of all information. We should not spread news, decide, or act before investigating.

🌱 TO BECOME A BETTER PERSON

By thinking critically and validating information before acting, I develop my creativity, curiosity, and I reinforce my problem-solving skills.

♡ WITH THE HELP OF ALLAH

O, Allah! Give me the patience and intelligence to assess any situation.

END WITH AL-HAMDOULLILLAH ☾

♡ ♡ ♡ **DAY # 30** ♡ ♡ ♡

We sincerely hope that you enjoyed this book.
We worked diligently to bring to light the essential values of Islam to help our children fulfill their highest potential.

If you believe we can further enhance our content, please don't hesitate to contact us at :

info@goodheartedbooks.com

Otherwise, feel free to rate and share your review.

Thank you!

Printed in Great Britain
by Amazon